Don't Make Art, Just Make Something
the process, struggle, and vital importance of getting started

Miranda Aisling

Copyright © 2013 by Miranda Aisling
All Rights Reserved.

Cover Design by Union Press
Somerville, MA
www.unionpressprints.com

ISBN: 978-0-615-82036-1

www.DMAJMS.com

For Mairead

*Because reading anything is better than sitting
and worrying that you're reading the wrong thing.*

Have you ever noticed that whenever someone does something particularly well, we call it art?

The thing is, if we're always trying to make art, we miss out on everything else we can make.

what you're holding

Right now you're holding something in your hands.

It's not a distillation of years of thought, experience, and research, or a collection of what my grandfather calls "pearls of wisdom."

But it is something.

More importantly, it's something that *I made*.

What you'll read in this book is what I discovered as I was writing it, as I was proving to myself that it's never too early to get started.

content

something
defining art
what's the problem with making art?
just make something
under the glamour
what comes from nothing
the i's
inertia
inhibition
from 0 to 60
now what?
get started *now*
how this book got started
from surviving to creating

a bit of backstory
examples vs. exceptions
two somethings
applying to college
why not?
what people hear
what I should be
on being terrified
my dirty little secret
nanowrimo
the second, third, and fourth
the first and the awful
it's never too early

what tests have taught us
testing culture
all the little bubbles
erased abilities
question everything
where have all the questions gone?
predigested bits of information
sit still, be quiet, and listen
"I swear! It really was an alien!"
just *try*

shame
artistic vs. creative
the creative type
copy-cats
a constant companion
frequent failures
fail magnificently
test score factories

what we can do about it
real preparation
jump anyway
that last fast curveball
the first something
our time
scattered
good people
the greater community
just send it
the perfect title
the unanswered
creative habits
write every night
nineteen-and-counting
techniques
losing track of time
change the game

what it means to be passionate
a windmill in a hurricane
the accidental artist
drawing class
what we can learn from artists
awkward mules
passion vs. dedication
satisfaction

what's the point?
how to choose something
join the conversation

something

defining art

Let's start with **art**.

It's a confusing word.

There are "*the arts*," as in music, theater, dance, storytelling, and visual art.

There is "*art*," as in specifically visual art: paintings, sculptures, and drawings.

Then there is "*art,*" as in something that is done particularly well: The art of cooking, the art of writing, the art of shaving.

This is the kind of art that I'm talking about.

what's the problem with making art?

In the long run, there's nothing wrong with making art. In fact, as an artist myself, I'd say it's quite important.

But nobody starts out by making art.

We start out with piles of crumpled sketches, machines that fall apart when touched, and cramps after two minutes of jogging.

We've been raised to shoot for the stars, but nobody ever told us that we're lucky if we manage to even get off the ground on the first try.

That **nobody** reaches the stars in one shot.

So the problem isn't with making art, the problem is what we do before we're good enough to make it.

just make something

I wish you could hear my voice when I explained this, because then you would understand.

In the title of this book I'm not saying, "just make *[shrug]* something."

I'm *begging* you to just make something.

I'm talking something real, something you can be proud of, something that inspires you.

I firmly believe that if we go out and make *that* kind of something every day, we will start making art without even realizing it.

under the glamour

These somethings are the uncelebrated side of **passion**.

They form the hours upon hours of unrelenting dedication that over time become innovation.

As Picasso said, "Inspiration exists, but it has to find you working."

The time we spend hunched over pottery wheels, plunking out scales, practicing equations, and running drills is not *glamorous*.

It's **real**.

what comes from nothing

Nothing happens when we do nothing.

Even less happens when we sit and worry about what we're going to do instead of doing it.

But when we do *something*, anything can happen.

You could be imaginative all day long without anyone noticing. But you would never say that someone was creative if that person never did anything. To be creative you have to actually do something.

It involves putting your imagination to work to make something new, to come up with new solutions to problems, even to think of new problems or questions.

-Sir Ken Robinson
author of The Element
and Out of Our Minds

the i's

Two things can get in the way when someone tries to start something:

inertia

and

inhibition

inertia

Inertia is a basic resistance to change:

> *an object at rest stays at rest while an object in motion stays in motion unless an external force is applied.*

Physics itself is telling us why it's so easy to stay sitting on our butts as the world goes by. It takes a great deal of force to get up off the couch.

A great deal of **force**, or a lot of *little somethings*.

You'd think that for an object that's already in motion, inertia is great: once we get ourselves moving, we should just keep chugging along.

Except that every day is a constant series of external forces being applied against us.

Often, the biggest are our own inhibitions.

inhibition

There are three types of inhibition:

1.) What we learn from *society*.

2.) What we learn from our *family*.

3.) What we develop *ourselves*.

This last type of inhibition is the most dangerous because it comes from inside. It's the little part of our own voice that tells us, for whatever reason, that we aren't good enough.

The best way to prove these inhibitions wrong is by actually doing something.

Because nothing shuts up *inhibition* like **action**.

The way to get unblocked is to lose our inhibitions and stop worrying about being right.

-Paul Arden
author of It's Not How Good You
Are, It's How Good You Want To Be

from 0 to 60

There's a branch of behavioral psychology that helps people face their fears by exposing them to increasing amounts of what frightens them.

This technique can also work to battle both *inertia* and *inhibition*.

Very few people can go from the couch to their dreams immediately.

The ones who do often don't inspire us, they make us think that all we have to do is sit and wait for our luck to come. When it doesn't, we don't second-guess the circumstances, we second-guess **ourselves**.

But we all have the ability to do *something*, even if it's just a small something.

Over time, through hard work and dedication, these small somethings can pile up high enough that we can push past even inertia and inhibition.

now what?

When I was a sophomore in college I was sitting at lunch one afternoon with my friend Alex, who was about to graduate. She looked up at me over the dirty dishes and said, softly, "I'm twenty-three and I've never done anything but school."

Most of us have had this realization at some point, that we spend the first two decades of our lives preparing to make something *later*.

We study for tests to get the grades to get into schools to get degrees that *might* get us the job we're **supposed** to want.

Then, once we make it through all that, we stand at the end of our education and look out into life only to realize that no one ever told us *how* to actually get started.

get started *now*

The first time we try to make something shouldn't be when we're done with school.

And, actually, it's not.

As children we create every day, building entire worlds out of nothing but a few scraps of paper.

But somewhere between kindergarten and college we stop.

Why?

Instead of preparing students for what *might* come later, why don't we encourage them to start by making something **now**?

Why don't we tell them that it's never too early to get started?

how this book started

Like most projects, this book started out as just an idea.

I wanted to start a Creativity Training Program that could be provided as professional development to adults.

I thought about tailoring it for doctors, lawyers, business people, or teachers, but I felt like I didn't have enough information or experience to do that.

My discouragement was, in the end, my inspiration.

As I began to feel the fatal tug of **reality**, the slow start of acceptance that I *wasn't good enough yet*, I realized that fighting that discouragement is exactly what I want to do.

And so I decided to write a book.

from surviving to creating

When I first started, these pages were a disorganized jumble of too many ideas. In fact, they stayed that way for most of the time I was writing them.

It was only by writing—by actually *trying*—that my jumble of ideas became the book you're holding.

This book **is** my something.

I'm writing it in order to prove that we *can* do this, that we *can* make something.

Because it's only by actually making something that we will move from *surviving* our lives to **creating** our lives.

a bit of backstory

examples vs. exceptions

There are plenty of books and workshops out there that tell people having a midlife crisis that it's *never too late* to start something.

But there is almost nothing that tells those of us just getting started that it's **never too early**.

In fact, quite often we're told the opposite: that we're only good for menial chores because we're too young and don't have enough experience,

that all we can do now is prepare ourselves for what will come later.

The people who prove this wrong aren't held up as **examples**, they're pushed aside as *exceptions*.

two somethings

When I was thirteen I did two things that made it possible for me to write this book:

1.) I applied to college.

2.) I self-published my first novel.

applying to college

Despite warnings and concerns from everyone with an opinion—which was *everyone*—when I was in eighth grade I sent in my application to an early entrance program at Mary Baldwin College.

If I didn't get in it wouldn't matter; I would just continue on the normal path from eighth grade to ninth grade.

But if I did get in... well, I actually didn't know what that would mean.

why not?

Less than a year later, three weeks after my fourteenth birthday, I began my freshman year of college.

For two years I walked the line between terror and exhilaration.

I had made one of the hardest decisions that I will ever have to make, and there was a strong possibility that I had decided **wrong**.

And yet I did it.

Why?

Because I wanted to believe that it wasn't too early for me to get started.

what people hear

I've spent a long time struggling with the different ways that people hear my story.

Sometimes people hear about a person who's done something different and the first thing they think is, "If *they* can do it, that means I can do it!"

But other times that person is just shrugged off as an exception.

I am an exception, but I shouldn't be.

what I should be

I should be just one student amongst millions who were given the opportunity and encouragement to make their education work for them, who learned how to create their lives instead of just surviving them.

But instead, I find myself in a slim minority.

My education started at the Long Ridge School, an elementary school that didn't give grades, where science class was catching frogs, and art class was drawing fellow students standing in the middle of the table striking ten second poses.

This strong base allowed me to take a huge risk: to skip high school.

A risk, it turns out, that allowed me to retain my deep-seated love of learning and to discover and pursue an impassioned purpose while everyone was still expecting me to be sneaking out to drink and party.

on being terrified

When I left home at fourteen to go to college, I used up all the courage I had.

When I was seventeen, I finished college and began my adult life. I got an apartment, a job, and became financially independent.

Thanks to my college experience, I knew I could do it, but I was still scared witless.

Now I'm finishing my master's degree and using this book to start my career as a writer, speaker, and teacher focusing on the importance reconnecting art and education to daily life.

I wish I could say that I'm done being scared, but I do my best to always be honest.

A great deal of talent is lost to the world for want of a little courage.

>-Sydney Smith
>17th Century
>English writer

my dirty little secret

Although I'm not done with fear, I am done thinking that I'm too young to count.

As someone who is constantly doing things "*too early*," I have been embarrassed, indignant, lonely, and excluded.

For years now, my age has been my dirty little secret. Thanks in part to my height, most people began assuming that I was in my twenties when I was fourteen, and I generally let that happen.

Only now, with the safe protection of my older age, am I starting to own my story.

nanowrimo

The second thing I did when I was thirteen was write and self-publish my first novel.

For the first time I participated in National Novelist Writing Month, a program that sets a goal of writing a 50,000 word novel in a month.

That was the first book I self-published and I thought that it was absolutely incredible and would make me famous.

(Spoiler: it didn't.)

I didn't revise it or do any formatting before I sent the document off to Lulu.com because I was just *too excited*.

For three weeks I checked the mail constantly until finally it came:

a book with *my* name on the cover.

the second, third, fourth, and fifth

It took a year and a half for my pride to wear off and embarrassment to set in. After that I refused to let anyone see the awful writing in my first book.

And yet, since then I have self-published four books.

The second and third I let family and friends read with careful explanation that I wrote them when I was fifteen and sixteen.

The fourth I actually sent out to a few friends and asked for feedback.

The fifth is in your hands.

the first and the awful

Six years later, I can see that writing a book when I was thirteen was pivotal to writing *this* book now.

If I dug deeper I could tell you about the hand-written storybooks I made when I was in kindergarten and the plethora of unfinished chapter books I wrote throughout elementary school that made it possible for me to write that first book.

If I hadn't made that first awful book when I was thirteen, the thought of writing this book would never have even occurred to me.

it's never too early

Like every person at every age, I have doubts. For example, it's possible that the only people to ever read this book will be the ones I personally beg to.

But even if that's true, no one can ever take this book away from me. They can never again tell me that it's too early for me to write a book.

Because this book **is** my something.

When I started I was completely unprepared to write it. If I hadn't started, I would still be unprepared.

Only now, after actually *finishing* it, am I sure that I can do it.

As Michael Landon said, "Ready, Fire, Aim."

what tests have done

I.

How do I begin?

Nobody tells you that.
They show up to our graduations,
say a proud congratulations,
and for a day it feels like we've done everything.
But then the next day comes,
and the next,
and suddenly it's not exciting but terrifying
as we look out at our lives and realize
the time has **come**
and we're not ready.

We stand here
on the last piece of the past
looking out at the vast future
ready to jump from the springboard of our education
into the world,
only to realize that we won't spring that far.
We look down into the chasm that separates where we **are**
and where we **want to be**
and there are no guides,
no bridge to get across,
and that's when we see, as if for the first time,
that our two decades spent crammed at desks
prepared us only to pass tests that don't even matter once
we're done with them.
The reality that our education and profession are so disconnected,
that the mess we're in is **expected**,
knocks us to our knees
as we fight for footing on the precipice
of everything.

So how do we begin?

testing culture

Learning is about *creation*.

Unfortunately, the education world has been taken over by tests and over-preparation instead.

The testing culture has grown since the educational reforms in the 1980's and continues with No Child Left Behind.

This testing culture, created in *boardrooms* instead of *classrooms*, has disconnected education from students' lives.

People learn better when they can connect to what they're learning. Fractions, for example, were much easier to understand when my class was dividing up a bag of skittles.

But standardized tests are fundamentally **disconnected**.

The only reason for the existence of standardized tests is to provide a ranking system. Not to teach, not to inspire, simply to equate and evaluate.

all the little bubbles

Thanks to the rise of standardized testing, teachers are required to spend most of their time preparing students to fill in little bubbles on an answer sheet instead of teaching them to enjoy the process of learning itself.

Everyone learns something at school, and what students learn can and does help them. But what they *don't* learn is just as important.

What they don't learn is that whether they pass with flying colors or fail more completely than any student before them, trying to make something is worth it.

The school as a means of education was to me a complete blank.

-Charles Darwin
an English scientist

erased abilities

It wasn't until I was out of the educational world that I realized how disconnected it is from the professional world.

I was good at school, by which I mean I have always been a good test-taker. Yet somehow I still wasn't prepared for life outside the system.

This is because there are five essential abilities that the testing culture erases:

- questioning
- creating
- copying
- trying
- failing

It's because these abilities were erased that many of us have such a hard time just making something.

question everything

Being able to question is the ability to see something from a new angle, to challenge an assumed answer.

If we approach it right, every statement can be made into a question.

> *e.x. Can every statement be made into a question?*

Why does this matter?

Because questions create more questions while statements end conversations.

where have all the questions gone?

And yet, in most schools there is only one question:

> *"What's the answer?"*

because that's all that tests are looking for.

As Michele Moses and Michael Nanna explain in their article on testing culture, "Test scores are used to determine educational progress, evidence of learning, teacher evaluations, school quality, and high school graduation, among other things."

So basically, tests run the show.

predigested bits of information

Our test-based system doesn't leave room for the discovery and invention of new answers to new questions.

By learning to not ask questions and being fed predigested bits of information instead, too many students leave school not knowing how to find their own answers.

As the author and Stanford professor Tina Seelig says, "curiosity is a fragile thing," and the standardized testing system is smashing it.

If I had an hour to solve a problem and my life depended on the solution, I would spend the first fifty-five minutes determining the proper question to ask, for once I know the proper question, I could solve the problem in less than five minutes.

-Albert Einstein
a German-American scientist

sit still, be quiet, and listen

When there is always only one right answer, students never have to think of a solution on their own.

Instead of being encouraged to take risks and think of new things, students are forced to sit still, be quiet, and listen because otherwise they won't pass the test.

As my friend Katie put it, throughout her education all she thought was: "Tell me what I need to do and I'll do it."

Standardized testing and the strict curriculums that go with it are forcing **independence** and **initiative** out of America's students.

No wonder it's so hard for us to get started.

"I swear! It really was an alien!"

This is especially true in the **arts.**

Before they get into school, kids are creating everyday. They sing, act, draw, dance, and tell stories, interacting with the world every way they can.

Young-Ha, a famous Korean writer, says that "the moment kids start to lie is the moment storytelling begins. They are talking about things they don't see. It's amazing. It's a wonderful moment. Parents should celebrate!"

Instead, kids are often discouraged when it comes to their creative expression.

Schools are being forced to cut the arts programs that, as the database ArtsEdSearch specifies, can teach students the **creative thinking**, **critical thinking**, and **problem solving** skills that would help them figure out how to navigate the professional world.

We don't grow into creativity; we grow out of it. Often we are educated out of it.

-Sir Ken Robinson
author of the Element
and Out of Our Minds

just *try*

One of the inspirations for this book came from a group of thirty middle schoolers that I worked with earlier this year.

The day they came into my class I had an hour to get them to draw and three of them wouldn't even *touch* their pencils.

By the end of the period, I managed to convince each of them to at least draw something.

One drew a great picture but erased it halfway through, one drew a quick, half-hearted sketch, and one only drew a circle.

shame

It's a sad day when getting a kid to draw a circle is an accomplishment even though five years earlier they would have drawn anything without hesitation.

But as we grow older parents, teachers, friends, siblings, TV shows, and strangers teach us to be afraid of trying.

They tell us to be careful, to hesitate, to learn what is worth our effort, to consider what other people might think, to make sure we're ready first.

They teach us **shame**.

It doesn't take long to learn—embarrassment is a quick teacher—and soon enough we're too scared to even pick up a pencil.

artistic vs. creative

Part of the fear of pencils comes from the fact that most people believe that being **artistic** and being **creative** are the same thing.

This means that if they've been told that they aren't good artists, they think they aren't creative at all.

The Oxford Dictionary defines creative as "*involving the use of the imagination or original ideas to create something*" and artistic as "*having or revealing natural creative skill.*"

As you can see, to be artistic we have to be creative, but to be creative we don't have to be artistic.

To be creative, all we need is the courage and the confidence to make something.

the creative type

There are two types of people:

The ones who believed the person who told them they weren't creative,

and the ones who didn't.

I'm not sure if you noticed, but not being creative isn't an option.

>You may not know it,
>
>you may not use it,
>
>but you **are** creative.

copy-cats

Everything we use has been conceived of and invented by someone, including this sentence which up until that comma was originally written by Tina Seelig.

But because education is controlled by standardized tests instead of inspiring teachers, **copying** is the same as **cheating**.

While teaching, I've taken up the art teacher's mantra that copying is the best form of flattery. But that doesn't go far with students who have been trained to believe that copying is basically a sin.

And yet, one of the best ways to get started is to be inspired by someone else's work and then to try it out for ourselves.

True, people do look for something new, but sometimes it's just something new to copy.

To be original, seek your inspiration from unexpected sources.

-Paul Arden
author of It's Not How Good You
Are, It's How Good You Want To Be

copy honestly

To copy well, we have to copy *honestly*.

Cheating off of someone else's test and plagiarizing are not the same as making our own version of a famous art piece.

We have to teach the difference between *copying* and *cheating* by encouraging students to copy and to give credit.

As the author and artist Austin Kleon writes, "a wonderful flaw about human beings is that we're incapable of making perfect copies. Our failure to copy our heroes is where we discover where our own thing lives. That is how we evolve."

a constant companion

But there is something even worse than copying when it comes to tests:

Failing.

Really, take a minute to think about it. The whole testing culture is set up to avoid failure because we've made failing into the **Educational Armageddon**.

This excessive fear and punishment of failure makes it nearly impossible for anyone to start *anything*.

And yet, outside of the school system, most people would probably agree with the entrepreneur and venture capitalist Mir Imran when he says, "Failure is a constant companion, and success is an occasional visitor."

The messy, brutal reality is that failure is simply part of the deal.

frequent failures

We can't control the fact that everyone will fail at some point in their lives, but we can control our attitude towards failure.

Failure is a chance to learn, a reason to do something again and do it better.

You may not agree with me, but a lot of other people do:

Failure is only the opportunity to begin again more intelligently. -Henry Ford

Success is going from failure to failure with no lack of enthusiasm. -Winston Churchill

Of the 200 lightbulbs that didn't work, every failure told me something that I was able to incorporate into the next attempt. -Thomas Edison

Ever tried. Ever failed. No matter. Try again. Fail again. Fail better. -Samuel Beckett

And don't forget:

I haven't failed, I've had 10,000 ideas that didn't work. -Benjamin Franklin

I think I've made my point.

fail magnificently

All of us will fail at some point.

All we can do is make sure that when we do, we do it magnificently, that we fail like no one else has failed before.

Because sometimes failure can be just the something we need to get started.

Being prepared isn't a matter of how much you practice. It's about knowing that even if you fail, you won't give up.

-John Maeda
president of Rhode Island School of Design

test score factories

Schools should be this incredible place where students can go to begin to make sense of the world. For a lucky few, that's true.

But for many, schools are testing factories intent on molding students into nothing more than high test scores.

Mihaly Csikszentmihalyi, an influential positive psychologist, warns us that "the universe was not designed with the comfort of human beings in mind."

He forgot to mention that neither were schools.

To enjoy the incredible opportunity of education, students need to be taught to question everything, create constantly, copy honestly, try relentlessly, and fail magnificently.

Then they'll be able to actually make something.

what we can do about it

II.

We aren't starting our lives today, y'know,
that already happened, years ago,
thanks to the fight our mothers won.
A fight not to the death but for a life,
for **our** lives.
So don't disrespect their accomplishments by saying
you're just getting started,
cause the hardest fight is long over
and all we have to do is keep going to prove ourselves worthy of the victory.

We just have to go for it,
even when we don't know what **it** is
even when we've been flying on empty for so long it feels like we're just falling and we damn well better make something before we hit the ground.
We may land on our feet,
or flat on our face,
but either way we can stand up and say,
"I did that,"
And, y'know, it doesn't matter whether we're pointing at a goal we accomplished or a crater in the ground,
because it's **still something**.

Just imagine if we could all say that every night,
think of all the things we'd do,
of all the things we'd get right.
In fact,
we should make it a habit to do something everyday
just so that before the sun goes down
we can point at what we made
and say, "I did that."

"**I** did that."

real preparation

Tests and over-preparation, it turns out, actually aren't the best way to prepare. *Real* preparation comes from **action**.

Was I prepared to write this book when I started?

Not a chance.

But as I was writing I found what I wanted to say, and because of that I could read the right books and chose the best words to say it.

Only now that I'm done would I say that I'm ready to write this book.

Thankfully, I decided to start *before* I was ready.

jump anyway

There's an old saying that goes,

> *"Look before you leap."*

Generally, this is good advice, particularly in regards to safety. The problem is, once we look at how far we'll fall, we're usually too scared to actually jump.

In response to this specific, irritating saying, I wrote a folk song which ends with the phrase,

> *"I look before I jump, but I'll jump anyway."*

You see, no one knows what the world will look like in five years, let alone in the seventeen years that will pass before this year's kindergarteners graduate college.

So the best thing we can do is accept that we aren't ready and do it anyway.

that last fast curveball

This is the hardest part: starting when we aren't ready.

But it is also the *most important* part.

I don't know about you, but I *hate* not being prepared. I want to walk into a room knowing that I can own it.

Sometimes this works, but often that feeling of total-preparation is just overconfidence.

There is no such thing as being 100% prepared. We can get pretty close, but there's always that last fast curveball to prove us wrong.

It may or may not come, but if it does suddenly we learn what we should have known all along: that we weren't ready.

And if we don't know how to deal with not being ready, that curveball can knock us out.

the first something

The only way I've found to get myself started when I don't feel ready is by telling myself that the first something doesn't really matter that much.

My first book? *Just something I did to prove that I could.*

Applying to college at thirteen? *Just something I did to see if it was actually possible.*

I trick myself into thinking that what I'm starting is not such a big deal.

I mean, anyone can do something small, right?

The best way to overcome this angst is to start by taking small chances first, to build your creative confidence.

-Tina Seelig
a professor at the
Stanford d.school

our time

Starting small is pretty much the opposite of Preparing-to-Start-a-Life.

Is it really any wonder that we don't know what to do next when we were prepared to start a *life* instead of, say, to get an apartment?

It's all incredibly overwhelming.

Just look at what we live with everyday: test-driven schools, debilitating student debts, economic recession, unhelpful degrees, politics that read like tabloids, and the longest war in American history.

We have had to relearn the real world skills that the testing culture taught out of us while trying to find work in an economy that *no one understands*.

There's a lot working against us. But then, there's a lot working against **everyone**.

All we can do is start with something small.

scattered

It also helps to build a group of people you can count on.

This is surprisingly hard to do.

When I went to college I left behind every person I had ever known.

For two years I floundered, lonely and unsure. It wasn't until I was a junior that I made true friends, people who are still some of the best friends I've ever had.

But then college **ended**.

Now my closest friends are in California, Louisiana, Washington, and Virginia while I'm in Massachusetts.

This means that I spend a lot of time on the phone.

And a lot of time alone.

good people

Our parents and grandparents had their church groups, rotary clubs, and YMCA memberships.

We have packed subway cars, pretentious coffee houses, and bars.

My friends from all over the country say the same thing: "*I have no friends here.*"

But if my friends are that spread out, and your friends are that spread out, there has to be some overlap.

Find it.

Make it if you have to.

Because good people are something we can't and shouldn't have to live without.

Often we need other people to help us recognize our real talents. Often we can help other people to discover theirs.

-Sir Ken Robinson
author of the Element
and Out of Our Minds

the greater community

But even once we manage to build a group of people, there will still be times when none of them can help us.

That's when we have to turn from our *direct* community to the *greater* community.

It helps to read books and articles, watch documentaries and short internet videos, look for lectures and events to go to, or even just keep up-to-date on today's headlines

By doing this we can find new ideas and people to learn from.

just send it

Earlier this year, as the idea for this book was just forming, I found the work of Ellen Winner. She studies the developmental psychology of arts and co-wrote the book, <u>Studio Thinking</u>.

Upon closer inspection, I saw that she is a professor at Boston College, fifteen minutes away, so I decided to try and contact her.

She not only responded to my email, she took the time to sit down and talk with me.

I took the subway to her office at Boston College and spent an incredible hour speaking with her about arts, education, creativity, and what I was planning to write.

That afternoon I decided that no matter how small a chance there was of someone responding, I would always at least *try* contacting them.

the perfect title

Around the same time, I did a quick Google search that turned out to be one of the most important inspirations for this book.

I was looking to see if the first title that I thought of using, A Crash Course in Creativity, was still available. It was to the point, understandable, and used a well-known phrase.

Perfect.

It was so perfect, in fact, that Tina Seelig had already written it.

The thing is, she's a Stanford professor with a Ph.D. in neuroscience who has been teaching longer than I've been alive.

But instead of being discouraged, I bought her book, read it in, and was inspired

It was because I couldn't use her title that I came up with Don't Make Art, Just Make Something, which, it turns out, is what I was trying to say all along.

With enhanced creativity, instead of problems you see potential, instead of obstacles you see opportunities, and instead of challenges you see a chance to create breakthrough solutions.

-Tina Seelig
a professor at the
Stanford d.school

the unanswered

This is not to say that everyone I have tried to contact has gotten back to me.

But I decided this year that I would send emails to anyone I think could help me even if I don't think they'll reply. Because if I try enough times, *something* is bound to happen.

And when I do get a response, it makes all those other times, where I check my email ten times an hour to no avail, worth it.

creative habits

Many creative people say that habits are bad, that they create drudgery and routine where we need spontaneity and change.

But what if we make something so often that creating *itself* becomes habit?

Then the nauseating anxiousness of creating can become more manageable.

If we choose something small, like taking a photograph, drawing a sketch, or writing down an idea, we can do it everyday.

With a simple creative habit like this, over time some interesting things start to happen.

write every night

For example, I have journaled every night since March 22, 2008. At the time this book was launched, that came to 1,897 nights.

My first ever journal entry was on February 3rd, 2001 in a Lisa Frank diary with purple penguins hugging on the front. It went like this:

> *Dear Diary,*
> *I when't to a baby shower today. It was Kristen's Mairead's skating teacher. It's 2:30 pm. I'm lisening to the Betles Please Please me Saturday February 3thrd 2/3/01 I'm bord. I think I'm going to wrighte a book.*
> *I think right now bye Diary.*

Because I was writing only when I felt like it, six years passed before I filled up that first journal.

That's when I realized that if I wanted to actually document my life I would have to write every night, because writing two weeks of events in an evening just doesn't work.

nineteen-and-counting

By now, this habit is so deeply ingrained in me that I can't go to bed without writing.

Honestly, I doubt anyone will ever want to read all nineteen-and-counting of my journals.

So what's the point?

Well, apart from knowing exactly what I did any day from March, 22, 2008 until now, journaling every night makes me practice writing, it strengthens my memory, and I'd say that after five years it's a damn impressive accomplishment.

I only write about a page each night and usually it feels like I'm not adding anything.

But over the course of five years that's become a lot of pages. And since I've already written that much in my journals, I knew I could fill the hundred pages of this book by applying the same habit:

Just write *something* every night.

techniques

Over time, due to my journaling habit and other writing habits, my writing has gotten much better.

Cal Newport, author of <u>So Good They Can't Ignore You</u>, writes about the importance of spending the time to develop a valuable skill.

"Great work," he says, "doesn't just require great courage, but also skills of great (and real) value."

He goes on to explain that you can develop these great skills by "focus[ing] on difficult activities, carefully chosen to stretch your abilities where they most need stretching."

Through my years of journaling, the misspelled boredom of a seven-year-old has developed into what I hope is a reflective documentation of my life.

losing track of time

There's this incredible feeling that comes when you start stretching yourself.

Dr. Mihaly Csikszentmilhalyi calls it "flow - the state in which people are so involved in an activity that nothing else seems to matter; the experience itself is so enjoyable that people will do it even at great cost, for the sheer sake of doing it."

Sir Ken Robinson, on the other hand, calls it "being in the zone" and says that "activities we love fill us with energy even when we are physically exhausted. Activities we don't like can drain us in minutes even if we approach them at our physical peak of fitness."

I don't have a fancy name for this feeling.

All I have is the knowledge that when I am doing something I love, something that challenges me and stretches me, I lose track of time.

I'm so completely encompassed by the experience that even the clock doesn't matter.

change the game

All the tests, the preparations, the expectations, and the pressures to Start-a-Life make it nearly impossible to start anything at all.

Sometimes it feels like we are set up to **lose**.

But even if that's the case, there's something else we can do instead of just giving up: *we can change the game*.

Figuring out how to start even when we aren't ready, building a supportive community, reaching out to our mentors, developing creative habits, and finding whatever it is that makes us lose track of time changes the game completely.

And once we've changed the game we can start to make something, even if we're not ready.

on being passionate

III.

Finding passion is a lot like falling in love
and I don't mean that in a good way.
I mean that in a gut-wrenching, heart-aching, throat-clenching,
spirit-breaking way.
We've all been told how it should happen,
how it should feel,
they say we'll be swept off our feet,
dumped in a fairytale,
and then we'll be happy.

The thing is,
passion isn't something you follow.
It follows **you**.
Dogging your every step
from now until oblivion,
driving you forward day after day
to do what you love even when you hate it.
And there **will** be days when you hate it.
Because passion isn't happiness,
it's **drive**.

It's a drive that runs so deep you can never turn it off,
that can be so miserable you wish you could tear it out of you
but you can't,
because it **is** you.

Because passion isn't only falling in love,
it's daily toil of being in love.
It's the afternoon arguments,
the evenings of silence,
the late night tears.
It's the creeping doubt,
the endless effort,
the constant demand.
It's the moment you look at your lover standing there beside
the teapot you were arguing about two days ago

and you think,
"Oh, **this** is what everyone was talking about."
And for that day love comes freely
and passion is easy.

But those days,
the ones when clouds fly down from the sky
just so that you can walk on them
do not come often.
So cherish them.
Remember them when you have to show up the next day
even though the clouds are gone.
Because passion is worth working for.
It is a fire that runs through your veins,
not caring whether it's warming you or eating you alive,
but filling you either way.
It is a lifetime of dedication
with sparks of inspiration that are almost like the fairytales,
but **better**.

a windmill in a hurricane

I am a *deeply* passionate person.

As such, I've noticed that being passionate is not necessarily fun.

In fact, often it's quite miserable.

If you run into me at the right time I'll be spewing ideas, talking a mile a minute, and you may have to duck because I'll probably be gesticulating like a windmill in a hurricane.

That's what I like people to see, because that's the fun part. Exhausting, but fun.

But that's far from the whole picture.

the accidental artist

I became an artist by accident.

The only reason I started my art degree was because in my first semester of college two classes conflicted so I dropped one and picked up Art 111.

Although I was always very creative and loved my art classes, I never thought I could be an artist because I wasn't any good at drawing.

I showed up a week late for my first college art class and I vividly remember standing in the hallway, wondering when they would all find out that I wasn't a *real* artist.

drawing class

I knew my brief stint as an artist would be up when I had to take Drawing I.

There was this one girl in my class who was an absolutely incredible drawer. For one memorable assignment she came in for half an hour, drew a perfect skull, and left.

I, on the other hand, spent hours working and reworking my paper and it was still barely recognizable.

The next day my instructor, Paul Ryan, took one look at my drawing and loved it.

"You have such a strong composition here," he told me as I sat, transfixed in that hard plastic, paint-spotted chair. "And the *texture*, you're great with texture, Miranda. I want to see you push that more."

After that class I stopped comparing my weaknesses to others' strengths and my fate as an artist was sealed.

what we can learn from artists

Despite the reputation that artists have for being disorganized and irresponsible, a lot of what I've learned from them is actually quite practical.

This is because the artistic *reputation* is quite different from the artistic *reality*.

On most days, an artist's studio isn't full of inspirational new masterpieces waiting to be discovered. Instead it's piled high with scraps of paper covered in partial ideas and piles of paint that are the wrong shade of purple.

The truth is, at least half of the time even artists aren't making art.

But they are *always* making something.

awkward mules

What really makes an art piece are the **hours** upon **hours** of unnoticed, uncelebrated frustration spent just making something.

One of my favorite descriptions of this comes from Elizabeth Gilbert's TEDtalk, 'Your Elusive Creative Genius.'

"I'm not a pipeline," she explains, "I'm a mule and the way that I have to work is I have to get up at the same time everyday and sweat and labor and barrel through it really awkwardly."

Because being passionate isn't just doing what you love.

It's doing what you love even when you **hate** it.

passion vs. dedication

Although society likes to paint a romantic scene of the passionate artist who ruins their life in pursuit of their art, the reality is a little different.

The fiery, passionate inspiration that makes for such good movies is only part of what makes an artist. The other part, the one often left out of movie montages, is **dedication**.

Passion is what made me decide to write this book.

But dedication is why I'm lying here typing on a Saturday night even though I'm sick and all I want to do is take Nyquil and pass out.

The most important thing about art is work. Nothing else matters except sitting down everyday and trying.

-Steven Pressfield
author of the
War of Art

satisfaction

Passion is depicted as this magical elixir that makes life incredible. Once we find it, everything will be invigorating and we'll be happy all the time.

But this ignores the miserable, daily drudgery on the other side of passion. It's unglamorous, it's frustrating, and it's incredibly hard to get through.

And yet, *that's what passion is*.

Real passion comes from the **stubborn dedication** that fills the time between the sporadic days of breathless inspiration.

As I type the final pages of this book, my stomach is growling, my eyes keep wandering, and my fingers are itching to do something, anything else.

But there's also this deep sense of satisfaction and accomplishment because, through my passion, my dedication, I've **made** something

And all those somethings have become the book you're holding.

what's the point?

IV.

Why write a book that may never be read,
make a painting that may never be seen,
or run a mile when there's no race?
Because when the grades are done
and the directions are gone,
we are the only ones left to hold ourselves accountable.
But accountability is something that we haven't been taught
because everyone was too busy directing us,
too busy filling our minds with answers to a now forgotten
test to teach us how to do what's untested:
how to get started.

By the time we actually try
we've been tested so many times,
prepared for so long,
that we expect our first attempt to be **art**.
And when all we make is something our hearts are crushed
and uncertainty starts us down the path of just doing what we
have to do to get by,
and we start thinking it's enough to just survive.

But I want more than to **survive** my life.
I want to **create** my life.
And even though creating something is uncomfortable,
it's not impossible
as long as we can appreciate each piece along the way.
Each small something that takes us one step farther,
that makes us just a little bit better.
Because without the stepping stones
we will never get across.
We need to celebrate everything we do
as an accomplishment **in and of itself**,
even if it's only one part of a larger picture,
that one stepping stone is worth all the effort on it's own.
So don't make art,
just make **something.**

how to choose something

First, think about what would you like to do. Think big, impossible even. Give yourself a minute to dream.
ex. become a best-selling author

Break that dream down into its smallest, most inconsequential parts.
ex. writing well, finding a good story to tell, having a lot of readers, getting a publisher, etc.

Choose one of those parts and find a way to do it in less than fifteen minutes.
ex. do fifteen minutes of stream-of-thought writing.

Pick a good starting date.
ex. new years, your birthday, the first of the month, any Monday.

Find a place in your schedule where you can dedicate those fifteen minutes everyday.
ex. before bed, in the morning, at lunch

Do it until it's so natural that you can't imagine not doing it.

Then make it harder and repeat.

join the conversation

This book is just the beginning.

Visit www.dmajms.com to join in the conversation and share your something.

Keep up-to-date on upcoming workshops, lectures, and projects related to the book via:

> Twitter: @mirandaaisling
>
> Facebook: facebook.com/mirandaaisling

Last, but not least, pass this book on to someone else so that you can sit down, talk about it, and have a bit of human interaction.

Are you ready to start?

notes

something
- Ken Robinson. (2009). The Element. p. 67.
- Paul Arden. (2003). It's Not How Good You Are, It's How Good You Want To Be. p. 58.

a bit of backstory
- George Louis quoting Sydney Smith. (2012). Damn Good Advice. no. 119.
- Michael Landon quote told to me by Arnold Aprill.

what tests have done
- Ken Robinson quoting Charles Darwin. (2011). Out of Our Minds. p. 100.
- Michele S. Moses and Michael J. Nanna. (2007). "The Testing Culture and Persistence of High-Stakes Testing Reforms." p. 60.
- Tina Seelig. (2012). inGenius: A Crash Course in Creativity, p. 153.
- Tina Seelig quoting Albert Einstein. (2012). inGenius: A Crash Course in Creativity. p. 19.
- Young-ha Kim. (2013). "Be an artist, right now!" Translated by Clair Han.
- http://www.ted.com/talks/young_ha_kim_be_an_artist_right_now.html
- ArtsEdSearch, Cognitive Outcomes of Arts Education. http://www.artsedsearch.org/engaged-successful-students#cognitive
- Ken Robinson. (2011). Out of Our Minds. p. 49
- Oxford Dictionary Online. http://oxforddictionaries.com/us
- Tina Seelig. (2012). inGenius: A Crash Course in Creativity. p. 11.
- Paul Arden. (2003). It's Not How Good You Are, It's How Good You Want To Be. p. 88.
- Austin Kleon. (2012). Steal Like An Artist: 10 things nobody told you about being creative. p. 41.
- Tina Seelig quoting Mir Imran. (2012). inGenius: A Crash Course in Creativity. p. 158.

- Tina Seelig quoting Henry Ford. (2012). inGenius: A Crash Course in Creativity. p. 166.
- Paul Arden quoting Winston Churchill. (2003). It's Not How Good You Are, It's How Good You Want To Be. p. 122.
- Paul Arden quoting Thomas Edison. (2003). It's Not How Good You Are, It's How Good You Want To Be. p. 50.
- George Louis quoting Samuel Beckett. (2012). Damn Good Advice. no. 102.
- Paul Arden quoting Benjamin Franklin. (2003). It's Not How Good You Are, It's How Good You Want To Be. p. 50.
- John Maeda. (2011). Redesigning Leadership. p. 5.
- Mihaly Csikszentmihalyi. (2008). Flow: The psychology of optimal experience. p. 8.

what we can do about it
- Tina Seelig. (2012). inGenius: A Crash Course in Creativity. p. 173.
- Ken Robinson. (2009). The Element. p. 25.
- Tina Seelig. (2012). inGenius: A Crash Course in Creativity. p. 4.
- Cal Newport. (2012). So Good They Can't Ignore You. p. 51.
- Cal Newport. (2012). So Good They Can't Ignore You. p. 83.
- Mihaly Csikszentmihalyi. (2008). Flow: The psychology of optimal experience. p. 4.
- Ken Robinson. (2009). The Element. p. 93.

on being passionate
- Elizabeth Gilbert's TEDtalk, "Your Elusive Creative Genius"
- Steven Pressfield. (2002) The War of Art. p. 108.

Made in the USA
Middletown, DE
06 February 2015